BREAKTHROUGH

Changing the Pattern of Poverty

Copyright© Rosemarie Sánchez

First Edition: February 2020

ISBN: 9798644009923

All rights reserved

Publisher: Ediciones Autores de Éxito®

www.analiaexeni.com

Inscriptions

This book is decicated to you!

- To you, that life has hit you.
- To you, that life has abandoned you in the midst of the storm.
- To you, who have known how to get up after the falls with more brightness and light than the Dawn.

I toast for every victory you will get when your soul, mind and spirit come to connect in one entity!

You are the true success!

You have been created to succeed and to break all the barriers that separate you from that abundant life you deserve.

- To my father Roldan Sánchez.

You taught me that the greatest thing in life is SHARING.

Every day you dedicated yourself to loving your family, the queens of the house, your daughters.

You taught me how beautiful it is to LOVE and be LOVED.

- To my mother Ninela Sánchez.

You never doubted my abilities and you always put your hope and faith in everything I have undertaken on in my life.

You who know my weaknesses and my strengths.

- To my children, Luis Antonio and Gianna Paloma. Who are my life engine.

I write this book to leave a legacy of love in your lives.

They were and always will be the ones who pushed me to finish it. They are my greatest pride.

- To René Trujillo the father of my children.

Thank you for always keeping in mind that our children are to whom we owe ourselves.

Thank you for your friendship and all that our family represents, which are Luigi and Gigi.

- To my sisters who have been fragile but have always struggled to love more, live more and be more.

To Vanessa, Ninela and Rocío who are the treasures that identify me. To my sister Estefanía whom I admire. You are far, but not absent. God united us in a day of sadness but it marked our lives.

- To all the people who admire my work and together we walk paths of experiences every day.

We are more, we will be more and we will do more when we always live and remember that united all of us, we can always achieve it!

- To you, my dear reader.

Although we may not know each other in person, remember, you chose to be better, achieve more, and achieve survival goals by reading this book.

Endless Thanks and Blessings forever!

"When your thoughts have changed, your mind and soul always coordinate to achieve greatness".

Rosemarie Sánchez

INDEX/Content

- CHANGING THE PATTERN OF POVERTY. HEADING TO FINANCIAL FREEDOM.
- EVERY THOUGHT COUNTS.
- I WAS BORN WITH THE SPLENDOUR OF A STAR.
- A WISH IS NOT A GOAL.
- CHANGING NEIGHBORHOOD.
- CHANGE YOUR PERSPECTIVE AND IT WILL CHANGE YOUR LIFE.

Chapter 2   65

- YOUR RETROSPECTIVE MIRROR.
- A SMALL CHANGE IS NOT ENOUGH TO ACHIEVE ABUNDANCE.
- STRATEGIES TO ACHIEVE GREATNESS.
- VISUALIZE YOUR SUCCESS. CREATE YOUR REALITY.
- MENTALITY IS SPIRITUAL.

Chapter 3   99

- DAY-BY-DAY.
- YOUR SOUL SHOWS YOUR BRIGHTNESS.
- THE PEACE OF THE HEART FERTILIZES NEW SOIL.
- DO YOU MASTER THE ECONOMY?
- WHICH IS THE RIGHT ANSWER?
- MANIFEST THE CHANGE OUTSIDE OF YOU.

Prologue:

- ✓ What are your biggest dreams?
- ✓ Why haven't you accomplished them yet?
- ✓ What prevent you from advancing on the path of success and happiness?
- ✓ What's your biggest fear?

This book offers you all the answers that you have always sought to positively transform your life, but that you never found all together in one place.

Here they are! At last, you have them in your hands, but now it will be up to you to put them into practice **to take your life on an infinite path of unlimited growth.**

Success and happiness always go hand in hand, they are husband and wife, they are soul mates, same entity. So don't look for them separately. Both live in you!

Being successful and happy is a lifestyle and also a daily decision, but in order to achieve this, you will have to break all the barriers that isolate you from Eden.

You already live in paradise! But your false beliefs blind you and you can't see it. You keep walking through the desert searching an oasis and you have not realized that you are already in it.

This book is the key that will open you the doors of a new world where everything is possible and true.

✓ Don't wait for the solution to come from outside because it lives inside of you.

✓ Everything you need to be happy is beating right now in your heart.

✓ All the success you sought for years was always by your side.

Breakthrough it's your Aladdin's lamp. This book is the best gift you can give to yourself.

All those patterns of poverty that you have anchored will disappear with the practice of the fresh ideas that you will discover in this masterpiece.

Rosemarie is a woman who has gone through many challenges and misfortunes, but she

knew how to take advantage of every difficulty
to learn, grow and help other people.

She is an Unstoppable Woman who lives in
the light of her dreams and never in the
shadow of them.

The author experienced firsthand the
misadventures of a life full of adversities and
far from complaining, she took flight like an
eagle and learned to break all the barriers that
separated her from that dream life she wanted
and deserved. **She is not afraid of anything
because God is her ally!**

Like Rosemarie we can all conquer our
dreams. If we define our goals and work
passionately for them, sooner or later we will
be living that wonderful life that for other
people is only possible in fairy tales.

A bare tree begins spring with the conviction
that it will soon be covered in beautiful leaves

radiant of splendor; It knows itself perfect, lush and full of abundance; It does not worry about the dearth because it does not know the patterns of poverty; It does not worry about going to the bank to ask for a loan to buy green leaves for its empty tree branches.

Nature is wonderful and perfect!

Human beings are also, but in order to live a true life of abundance, it is necessary to *break patterns of poverty*.

Here are the tools to build your own universe!

Everything is possible if you have enough faith in yourself to conquer yourself.

Analía Exeni
Founder of: Ediciones Autores de Éxito ®
www.analiaexeni.com

Introduction:

I had to go through many deserts to understand that in my nature there was always and there is always success.

This book has grown with me for many years, since I lived in Venezuela and has accompanied me throughout my life until I came to Canada and settled in this beautiful land. It was motivated by all the adversities that I went through in my life, because they were the ones that inspired me to get ahead and the ones that gave me the necessary strength to grow. I had to train my thinking to be able to break those patterns where there is negativity; where there is selfishness; where there is heartbreak; where there is little self-confidence; where there is low self-esteem. All this is basically related to strengthening the spiritual world because it is there where true wealth is born, not outside.

I always had the conviction that we must break this pattern of thinking where there is the poverty of any kind, because poverty can be:

✓ spiritual
✓ emotional
✓ psychical
✓ soulish
✓ material

This book inspires you to break that pattern where there is poverty in any of its forms.

People begin to break down barriers when they untie what is binding their lives.

The bonds come from generation to generation. They come in the form of curses, of uncertainty, with negative words, with a poor mentality, with deficiencies of all kinds.

Breaking down barriers means to be free!

It means making your life a success and achieving unimaginable things. It is to develop yourself more as a person and transform yourself into a wonderful human being.

I have known the spiritual world a lot and I
have developed the physical world and I know
that the two are connected hand in hand.
When I decided to write this book I reflected
on myself. I thought of all the adversities that I
had to go through and I had to break;
therefore, I have been successful and have
reached goals.
When we break down barriers we are free,
because thought begins to change from
negative to positive, from dark to white, from
senseless to human, from heartbreak to love,
from low self-esteem to having high self-
esteem, from not believing in Christ to
believing with all your strength.

All the barriers that we want to break have to start with the soul, after the soul they go to the spirit and from the spirit they go to the mind and from the mind they become concrete on the physical plane.

In this book, I describe the *human self* the vision of how the human being is reflected in others. Many times by seeing ourselves reflected in others we are not able to break barriers, but if we trust ourselves more because we know where we come from and that God is with us, we will be motivated to meet and grow with dynamic, jovial, optimistic people. These kind of people who impact you with their positive energy, because energy is very important. It is created in the atoms and from the atoms, it becomes a particle and from the particle, it becomes something human and from the human it becomes ambiguous and

from the ambiguous it becomes excellence.
Everything is rhetorical. If you know the root of
the spirit, of the challenge of life that is
inculcated with the soulish roots, mental,
gender.

Philosophically, if we look at people who did
shocking things in their lives, challenges at the
human capacity level: like athletes, like
philosophers, like writers, singers; like people
with different abilities, for example, a blind
person. All of them **have broken barriers,
defying innumerable impossibilities
because they believed in themselves and
gave themselves the opportunity to prove
it.**

I'll tell you a story:
*One day, Thomas Edison as a child came
home from school and gave his mother a letter*

from the teacher. The puzzled and self-conscious mother began to cry and then read the letter aloud to her son Thomas, which read: "Your son is a genius. This school is too small for him, and there are no teachers here capable of teaching him anything. Please educate him by yourself."

After several years of his mother's death, at that time Edison was already one of the greatest inventors, reviewing the old memories that he had saved, he found the letter that caused his mother so much crying back then. The great inventor read the letter for the first time and was surprised because it said the following: "Your son is mentally retarded. We cannot teach him more at school together with other kids. Therefore, we recommend that you educate him yourself, at home".

This caused Thomas to be crying for hours.
Then he wrote in his journal:
"Thomas Alva Edison was a mentally retarded
child. Thanks to the dedication and
perseverance of his heroic mother, he became
one of the greatest geniuses of his time".

She broke all barriers and went beyond what
seemed impossible.

She saw so much light in her son that she
was willing to do anything to make that
light shine and illuminate the world.

As you have been able to see, life will
challenge you to break down barriers and
move forward. On that path that allows you to
fulfill your deepest dreams.

This book is the most powerful tool to
break all the barriers that separate you
from that spectacular life that you deserve.

Rosemarie

"Ask and it will be given to you; seek and you will find; knock and the door will be opened to you. For everyone who asks receives; he who seeks finds; and to him who knocks, the door will be opened.

Which of you, if his son asks for bread, will give him a stone?

Or if he asks for a fish, will give him a snake? So if you who are evil know how to give good gifts to your children, how much more will your Father in heaven give good things to those who ask Him!

Matthew 7:7-11

Chapter 1

CHANGING THE PATTERN OF POVERTY.

HEADING TO FINANCIAL FREEDOM.

> *"Don't be afraid to give up the good to go for the great".*
>
> *John D. Rockefeller*

Have you ever found yourself looking for a new goal? Or, have you had a great passion for an idea?

You must identify the great ideas that come to your mind and work passionately for them.

There is where the true success begins!

Anything that distracts you and keeps you from your goals is a serious mistake

Many people seek their own approval from others, but I guarantee you will always be disappointed.

Focus on your goals!

There are generations with new identities and new thoughts that drive them to obtain admirable and indescribable contingent responses; but many of us are influenced by the limitation of our responses; those that take us away from what we need to achieve.

However, success is very close: in a phone call, in an interview, and even in an educational seclusion experience.

All of this can be a vehicle for success.

Although your goal may have a conflict in your beliefs. You are still in control to continue and get a solution for your heart's desires.

I trust that more and more people understand the concept of *financial freedom*.

It is imperative to understand the difference between being an employee versus self-employment; being a business owner, or an entrepreneur; taking control of your finances to be an active investor.

What can two people do in a workplace where they interact with the desire to achieve success but know that they will not be able to achieve financial freedom?

It is very important that you have the determination to reach a goal of financial success finding solutions and simple concepts to advance until obtaining sources of *passive income* or *residual income.*

Passive income is generated by working hard with a clear objective towards true success, often making mistakes and learning from them; trying again and again with care, in constant action.

Generating an independent work system, not being an employee but an entrepreneur, a leader who pursues his dreams.

This is how *financial independence* is built, in a specific period of time, unlike being an employee all your life, which will never give you the opportunity to create *passive income* with a vision of long-term stability by reaping the money that was invested and worked; Where that money will be growing day by day, at every moment, even when you sleep you will be generating income because you have been able to build an unstoppable and consistent income stream.

You will find many ideas on this exciting topic in Robert Kiyosaki's book *Rich Dad's Cashflow Quadrant*, where you will discover a real teaching concept of financial intelligence.

Do you see yourself making investments?

You need a change of mentality to break the patterns of poverty in your mind and spirit.

When you are prepared to take great risks and have enough responsibility to move toward a clear goal of creating wealth, you will ambition irrational thoughts, but they will guarantee you success.

You must cultivate the ambition to empower other people, as we are all interconnected and we must seek to work as a team and leave the best for the next generations.

Human beings always create interpersonal relationships, admiring and inspiring each other. This allows us to combat fears and cultivate positive thoughts little by little.

You must understand that you are not alone on this ship, there are thousands of people, even millions, looking for the same thing as you.

I guarantee that by continuing to read this book you will know that it makes a lot of sense, because it will allow you to exchange your poor thoughts for thoughts of greatness.

I encourage you to transform your environment by motivating other people to create greatness.

Read, read, and read. You will not regret it for a second because the more teachings you receive; the more opportunities you have for success.

"You must begin to think that you are becoming the person you want to be."

David Viscott

Visit my website:

www.breakthroughrose.com

Subscribe to receive 30 minutes of personal training.

You'll also receive a calendar with inspirational quotes to remember that success is on the way!

EVERY THOUGHT COUNTS.

"Every thought that you have impacts you. By Shifting from a thought that weakens to one that strengthens..."

Wayne Dyer

Have you ever wondered why when you think of a moment of happiness and the positive episodes in your life, your heart beatings increase? It is because your soul answers, it is trying to associate more thoughts related to those positive emotions that can transport you to that moment and that situation.

It is the number of good thoughts you have that makes your life better and that you have good results in your projects.

This is possible and achievable with the daily practice of positive thinking.

The sea is infinite and blue, a color that brings calm and transforms the energy of adversity into freedom. This is the style of thinking that every human being seeks.

Some people can do this momentarily and transform their negative thoughts into greatness. The process is very simple, the idea is to direct your thoughts towards your achievements, towards your desires, towards your dreams; then add passion and enthusiasm to focus on them.

Everything you focus on grows, therefore you must focus on the positive and never on the negative.

I remember my vacations when I was a girl in Europe, they were days without problems, without burdens, just happiness, a wonderful time that I lived and enjoyed with my family. This is what your thoughts should do: live with the spirit of a child among adults, with a young heart, full of freedom.

My mother always taught me to be an authority, despite she was my mother and I was a little girl. This sense of authority allowed me to multitask and have a desire to learn more; feeling inside me the fervent wish that my mother was happy and proud of me.

Isn´t It that the thought that every human being is looking for in society? I am sure you know the answer is in your mind and soul.

Once you recognize your thoughts and understand how they affect your perspective, you will always choose think positive. Begin today changing every mistake that prevents you from developing the result to achieve success. You can do it through positive thinking. It's that simple!

"The way to be truly happy is to be truly human, and the way to be truly human is to be truly godly."

Jl. Envasador

Forget about thoughts of negativity. You have control and the ability to react or stay calm. Your imagination can become really sensitive, but once you return to that thought and the need to get an answer, you will demand in your spirit patience and understanding. If you focus on achieving the goal, despite mistakes and failures, throughout the process you can also change your mentality.

There is always a possibility from adversity, and from that possibility a path to find.

No human being can be perfect; do we agree on that? But the key to success is taking control and assuming your power, that human power that allows you to choose a motivating thought, that power that makes you go forward and break the barriers of negativity and scarcity.

You can try a particular dream or goal that is in accord with God, by His will in your life. Focus daily on your goal and you will see how soon you can achieve it.

"To achieve the impossible, it is precisely the unthinkable that must be thought".

Tony Robbins

Reward yourself with people who can take you to the next level of positive energy where your thoughts and experiences are continually growing.

Transform your energy and pour out your self-esteem! Manifest your knowledge, whatever it is; show your ability at a level where incredible people will guide you and show you the vehicle to success.

We are all worthy to criticize or praise our
attitude because our own judgment is largely
an agreement or opposition to our destiny.
Remember that we see two faces in the mirror:
the positive and the negative.

It will always be your choice to express
positive or negative emotions infecting
everyone around you.

I WAS BORN WITH THE SPLENDOUR OF A STAR.

"The two most important days of your life are the day you are born and the day you find out why".

Mark Twain

I was born in June 1980, it was a miracle for my parents and a manifestation of God. Since my mother suffered pre-eclampsia during her pregnancy, she was delicate from the seventh to the ninth month.

My mother called me Rosemarie because of a well-known pianist named Rosemarie Sader. Coincidentally, I was born and raised to be an artist. I studied music from the age of seven to sixteen and I sang in various choirs and musical groups. I also learned different instruments throughout my career, but a decision changed my destiny: I gave up. My parents' dream was for me to sing in concerts with the symphony orchestra, but, was it my dream? Maybe yes; in fact, it was something that could have been developed with great potential.

I gave up at the time because my thoughts and plans weren't as big as my dreams. Did I give up? No. I refused to give up!

Do I regret the decision to abandon one of my dreams when I was underage? Indeed!

But it is never too late to keep moving and keep fighting for a great future. My destiny is ahead and my dreams are not over yet.

In the title of this chapter I refer to the splendor of a star so that you understand that your life is like the star: brighter every day! Because a star never stops shining. There are times when even the moon tries to cover it, but still the star manages to stay awake, shining and giving power to the dark night. I definitely encourage you to shine in your life with positivism.

Statistics show that people who laugh for more than seven minutes a day have a longer life expectancy than people who experience anxiety throughout the day.

If you have a habit of being negative you will attract more negativity into your life, but if you are positive you will enjoy the positive people that you will attract like a magnet.

Millennials still cannot find answers to many questions, such as the future or the educational system. Why? Because they are digital natives, technology is their way of communicating. They live more in the present, but at the same time, they also have too many distractions. Lack of control in the use of technology makes people lazy to find solutions and new ideas to improve their quality of life and the one of their loved ones.

Every human being has the power to develop their full potential. Did you know that the mind only works at 7% of its capacity, even people who have a high level of IQ develop only 10%? Despite this, we are so brilliant that we can conquer anything in this life.

Through the years, I have taken care of my education, I have searched, listened, studied, and admired people who later became my mentors. I can guarantee you that the more I learn, the more I want to know. Sometimes, among friends, I have been nicknamed *curious*. At first, I did not understand why I was nicknamed like this, but after analyzing it I understood that it is because I tend to look for many ideas for a solution and a solution for many ideas. I need to break the pattern of poverty in my mind. We all need it because it is necessary to eradicate everything negative that has been instilled in us in the past. We need to be resistant to everything that binds us to a life of scarcity.

The human being is perfectly designed by the grace of God, with the admirable eyes of our Creator.

Your energy is the symbol of your inner attitude. Get out of your comfort zone, and look for more! Read more books, travel to more places, meet more people; accept everything that brings you more knowledge and information; look for tools to continue developing and allow you to improve your quality of life. Begin a plan, a goal, with the purpose of achieving the highest standards in your life.

I'm a star and I was born to expand, again and again, it's never too late!

"Education is an ornament in prosperity and a refuge in adversity."

Aristotle

Send me a message through my website:

www.breakthroughrose.com

You can sign on and get 30 minutes of free tutoring.

A WISH IS NOT A GOAL.

"A leader is a dealer in hope".

Napoleón Bonaparte

Where do you go or who do you turn to when you need to have hope?

Is it a wish or a goal what you want to achieve?

Have you often asked yourself these questions?

You are not alone! Many people look for answers that they never find.

Many people desperately want a change, depositing a great source of hope in their mind and spirit.

But any radical change begins with commitment, then, without the right amount of effort or paying the price of defeat, you don't create a journey where is posible to achieve a goal.

I speak to you from experience, because I have been an entrepreneur from a very young age. It was part of my dreams and choices, why did I choose to be an entrepreneur? I tell you why. My family was wealthy and involved with influential people in Venezuela. Where I was born we had a good and very comfortable life. My parents always wanted me to search more and they went out of their way to provide me with an education that showed me that real life is difficult, even when we were living a comfortable life monetarily.

You can travel to many countries, attend private schools, to take extracurricular classes, have beach properties, your own condo, etc.

I have always had aimed to compete to win and mainly to love myself.

Even though my life was incredibly good in terms of abundance, at school I asked my classmates to buy things for me, which in turn I bought and then sold to a larger quantity. Did I have the necessity to do that? No! I'm sure of that, but the desire to demonstrate that I was capable of doing so was greater than the general rule of staying in the comfort zone.

I had my needs covered, my parents provided me everything, but I knew I could prove to myself, that I could go one step further and do more for myself. It seemed like a lesson to me.

Life makes sense to me when I take risks to achieve a goal, not just a wish!

I always wished to have my own business, but that wish only became a great goal when I set myself the goal of going to Canada to study English. At first I was not in love with the English language, rather from French. I knew how to speak French before English. I was always avoiding the subject of learning English, although I knew with certainty that my dreams would be fulfilled outside of Venezuela, and Canada was my great goal.

Your purpose of life is far from where you feel safe, chances are if you're still there, you're risking your energy, your family, your position, and even your feelings. Get out of your comfort zone right now!

I wished to be someone better, and behind that wish was a higher goal and purpose. God was giving me the vision of a better future, even though I had not found everything on my trip to Canada, not even the ability to understand the magnitude of the change that would allow me to finally settle in a foreign country and begin a new chapter in life. All I saw was the risk I had to take and find my life's purpose, but once I was inside the great project that I created with the help of my parents and grandmother, I went forward with infinite faith.

I thank God that it was a goal and not just a wish, that He connected me with the people I needed at the right time and favorable for me, and I did His will and I did not care about the barriers that came out, because my faith was greater than them. God definitely gave me a lesson.

Every time you take a big risk in life, you will be facing a goal, not just a wish!

Read more:
www.breakthroughrose.com/topics/leadership

CHANGING NEIGHBORHOOD

"When we are no longer able to change a situation, we are challenged to change ourselves."

Viktor E. Frankl

A considerable amount of people seeks to move to a place where summer prevail, while other people seek to live in winter. The question is: What difference can that make if the spirit remains the same?

Families are changing patterns to get good news, looking for solutions to their needs, but, will that really change yourself?

I discovered that while moving and fighting against destiny, with new and fresh ideas, you breathe the adaptation of the morning sun every day.

I know that if my mind finds answers to my needs, but if the needs continue to grow, the perspective will change indirectly, is it for better or for worse? You have the answers. Once providence is seeking a goal, the direction of your needs and your own self will always be reversible.

My neighbor was a girl who was always looking for problems. Did I follow in her footsteps? I knew for sure that if the same thing happened to me, I would be lost, but the mistakes had reached their peak and it was time to change. Does this encourage a change of neighborhood? Is it okay to discriminate or go against it? Of one thing I am sure, it is never too late.

I want to go above the sky and find a solution for my mom, can I do that? I certainly can't. I can do it only if I can work on my own. I can guide you with this book. Do I have all the answers? Let's leave that to the will of God!

"The Oracle of one who listens to the words of God and knows the knowledge of the Most High, who sees the vision of the Almighty, who fails, but who has his eyes uncovered".
Numbers 24:16

A neighbor will light up your life once you allow it, they can try to seduce you by showing you their ways, but you will still make the decision according to your beliefs. You can easily look up or draw the past into the future if you allow

your own decisions to manifest by showing
space and time.

**The neighborhood is definitely a way to
describe who you are, your being, and your
surroundings. I'm sure you keep moving
towards success, step by step, maybe
sometimes slowly, but you move forward!
and that's the important thing because you
decide not to stop.**

A positive mind makes things always possible,
despite adversity and uncertainty, because
your spirit is accomplishing the process.

If human beings communicate more effectively
and focus our needs collectively, thoughts and
behaviors change throughout a process that
shows the magnitude of progress.

I deserve and you deserve time, matter, and space, working collectively for it.

- **Will it happen? Yes.**
- **Will it work? Yes.**
- **It's possible? Yes.**

You are the reason, the passion, the fervor, the love, and the admiration.

The processes you have, work and train, will be like a transparent glass, half full, half empty. Your philosophy and discipline are yours and will adapt to your financial needs if you achieve a different role, attitude or aptitude in actions. If you do this, it is sure to manifest itself favorably.

CHANGE YOUR PERSPECTIVE AND IT WILL CHANGE YOUR LIFE.

"Once we accept our limits, we go beyond them".

Albert Einstein

People complain most of the time about insignificant things that have no solution if you change your perspective and instead of complaining, you think about how to change the situation, you will be on the right path, in an acceptance process that will lead you to find the right strategy to free you from your problems.

If you are reading this book, I am sure that great opportunities will come to your life and you will not even notice it.

Don't try to control or manipulate every negative situation, rather change it for your benefit. What benefit can it be? I know for sure that you have the decision in your hands.

Eradicate fears in yourself, because you have wasted time, energy, and effort damaging the chosen path.

I had times where my soul was wasting energy in situations that I could not control, or only to change my point of view and twist the perspective in my favor. Part of this mistake wore me out and ruled my life unfavorably as I had not yet broken the pattern of thoughts of my mental poverty.

I encourage you to unite your soul with mine, in feelings, thoughts, and actions to obtain the results you want to achieve today, tomorrow and always.

Never cultivate thoughts of negativity that control who you are, because the ego will strike and perhaps the enemy will take advantage of your fall. Pursue Love, love God, and spread the word of wisdom with dignity to your loved ones, instead of wasting your energy on things that are not possible to solve at that particular moment.

In those difficult moments, you can do something different to feel better, such as energizing your body with physical exercise, going for a walk, reading, or just resting.

Always keep in mind that risks and failures are part of today and never of tomorrow.

I firmly believe that you should not condition your state of mind with anyone's actions, only with yourself. Dedicate your mornings to the daily routine of thanking for the small or big things that you have in your life. Communicate much more and often with your loved ones. The more love you give with intensity; life will give you back in the same way. We are used to following the crowd.

What is your purpose in life?

If you have the focus on your life purpose, difficulties will never be an obstacle to achieving your goals.

I recommend that you change one thing at a time to make favorable changes happen in sequence.

Change your perspective and it will change your life. Remove attention from problems and focus on the solutions.

My son Luis Antonio, who is only twelve years old, also my ten-year-old daughter Gianna Paloma are my source of blessing. Their attitudes and their gentle ways of showing their affection allow me to see the purity and the greatest love. They do not judge but contribute positively giving the best. That innocence that nests within their heart, it is the greatest blessing and that is what I focus on every day to thank and bless all the happiness that God has given me.

Focus today on everything that magnifies your life; discard negativism as garbage as part of your old self. Energize your body, mind, and soul in the chosen purpose that is your stigma.

"Never underestimate the Power of the Mind. Persist in creating new thoughts to prevent falling back into negative patterns. It is an ongoing struggle and you have to commit to winning if you are going to succeed".

Bob Proctor

Chapter 2

YOUR RETROSPECTIVE MIRROR.

"The real competition has to be with oneself".

Carl Lewis.

Mary chases victories while Paulo tends to see people's faults. Paulo had a disciplined life and a very good childhood. He traveled through many countries and practiced many sports. His vision of life is to always excel and win since he is a competitive and athletic man. However, Mary always lived her life struggling to recover from losses, feeling a lot of pain, but through life's experiences, she learned not to lose faith and gain one more challenge to continue her battles. On the other hand, Paulo as soon as he lost a game or was unable to resolve a friendly confrontation, his wings closed. Do you know why?

Paulo is always competing with someone else. Mary is always competing with herself.

This is the reason why a mirror is retrospective. You have the opportunity to start and end a battle, express your thoughts and love for good or bad reasons. You can also maintain a position of dispute or grow in miracles. You can fight against the enemy with self-love or end the dispute with hatred.

Poverty patterns grow in your mind with disputes, despair, pain, regret, guilt, confrontation, lawsuits, resentment, discontent, unrealistic goals, everything negative created throughout the time, years, decades, and never changes to improve.

Poverty is not based only on the physical plane, but mostly on the poverty that inhabits people's thoughts and minds.

If you had to identify yourself with one of the characters in this story, would you choose Mary or Paulo? You will agree that either can be a possible choice.

But if you had to choose just one, would it be a difficult decision?

The key is that you can realize what is wrong inside and outside of you, in order to identify what is developing incorrectly through time and years.

Time is unlimited. The false beliefs of human beings have created a limited time to put limits on your wings, but now your choice must be to let your wings rise to build a better future.

Your life can manifest itself for better or for worse. The pattern of your thoughts can continue on an excellent path or turn towards mediocrity. Create a commitment to choose positive change with small steps. Now is your chance to confirm and correct what is changing in yourself or you can complain. You need to remove from your old pattern everything that is wrong to correct the side of your mirror.

"The books that help you the most are the ones that make you think the most. The most difficult way to learn is easy reading; but a great book that comes from a great thinker is a ship of thought, loaded with truth and beauty".

Pablo Neruda

I feel like I'm talking to myself. Paulo needs changes today. At this moment he must build a new soul, mind, and thoughts. While Mary is turning her behavior into heartfelt changes in herself.

Love is a mirror that you face every day, every minute, every second, in a society that will increasingly challenge your own will.

A SMALL CHANGE IS NOT ENOUGH TO ACHIEVE ABUNDANCE.

"You must be the change you want to see in the world."

Mahatma Gandhi

Estela is a professional woman; she loves to read but not cook. She does her chores but she always puts off one thing: organizing her ideas with a systematic process, since it is difficult for her to stop the torrent of ideas and thoughts to organize them. She has discovered that among her decisions and opinions one thing is missing: love for her own choices, ideals, passions, life criteria; although her position to delegate her needs and find peace in herself is always questioned. She is very determined in her projects, although her husband most of the time doesn´t understand her. He believes that she has not done much, but she knows that he is wrong. Her husband thinks that she has to keep the house in perfect condition at all times. In this marriage a lot of emotional support is lacking and strong changes are coming.

How can you stop a wave that is about to crash into the ocean? This wave is of great size and has a heavy load. Realistically, we can always make a change, however, the change will flow if we MANIFEST our intentions for good. The action plan will succeed in conquering, depending on what our determination is about. If it is FOR THE GOOD of all, it has greater possibilities than the other way around.

Estela finds herself trapped in a life without any meaning, without the support of the family and mainly of the person that she believes should be by her side, her husband. Her reclusive nature is killing her inside; she tries to force the barrier of her mind and there comes a moment of peace to favor a change; she tries to calm down; she actively participates in everything she finds motivating to get out of chaos; she questions her own actions.

Why human beings always allow ourselves to be so hard in our intentions? Then comes our victim position toward whatever we plan to change, thinking negatively; instead of cultivating positive thoughts and making affirmations.

Devote your life to extract the positive in each situation. Change your mental position to rest and make sure that, although the process hurt and is long, you will also find a light outside that tunnel soon enough to bless with your experience to others who may face the same or a similar challenge to the situation that you have now.

It must be enough for you the action and reaction of your affirmation, the changes of the world and perhaps the active discipline to motivate and form a completely different atmosphere.

Victories are important to exalt the greatness of the human being, because by trusting the process, you will see the change indefinitely.

"Time changes everything, except something within us which is always surprised by change".

Thomas Hardy

Estela creates brilliant and shocking emotions to delight her audience. Her followers are passionate about her teachings. She manifests a powerful statement, which is certainly applicable to her life.

Is it possible that she can give what she does not possess? Her shocking words will also change whoever she meets on her way and whoever is willing to lead the design of actions and question her thoughts.

The decision is always edifying here and there. It will eventually work if your focus is on one goal.

You must develop your abilities to the fullest; to love all people and never give up on your dreams.

Your positive actions will surely provoke a wave of favorable changes to improve your quality of life.

You need to wake up from that wonderful dream where you are already everything you always dreamed of being.

THE ONLY REASON OF YOUR LIFE IS TO BE WHO YOU ARE! a wonderful creature that God designed for the greatest purpose:

TO HAVE A LIFE OF ABUNDANCE!

STRATEGIES TO ACHIEVE GREATNESS.

"Just as a bud is transformed into a beautiful flower and just as a caterpillar is transformed into a beautiful butterfly, in the same way we human beings have enormous potential to transform ourselves into everything we can dream of. For that reason, DREAM BIG AND YOUR RESULTS WILL BE AS BIG AS YOUR DREAMS".

Analía Exeni

Do you remember your pure and excellent childhood? A child who dreamed big, but at the same time without thinking so much about the future? Do you agree that, as you grow older, boundaries begin to affect you because of your parents' wrong words or orientation? Did they make you think you're not good enough to play sports, run a business, or be a good friend? These are all perceptions of them. Your mind is being conditioned by the beliefs of those people; but remember, it is you who must create a strategy to change and make a difference. What can you do in these circumstances? You have two options:

1. **Stay with those false beliefs buried in your unconscious mind.**
2. **Condition your mind to change negative beliefs for others that favor you.**

The second option means that you must reprogram your self-belief in yourself.

**Beliefs need a change of consciousness;
Does it sound deep? Yes, it does!**
Let me further explain the process you have to
follow as I search for the right words.

How should you think? You must bring the
thoughts into the conscious process; realize
what is really inside of you; recognize your
talents, your values, your needs, and the love
that flows towards what you want in life. You
are in fact a channel, a passage, an
agreement with your mind here and now.

Do you believe me? Does it sound familiar to
you? Does it make sense?

*"Change your life today. Don't gamble on the
future, act now, without delay".*

Simone de Beauvoir

Do you see what it really takes to make a difference? They are only continuous, progressive actions. It is everything that gives you abundance, manifesting a new reality for you and for each person who is influenced by your authority. Who is right between authority and the discomfort of transformation in your mind, spirit and soul?

How much discomfort can you bear? The size of it is the answer to your goals and perhaps your dreams.

"What you are today is the result of past decisions and choices. What you are tomorrow is a consequence of today's actions".

Swami Vivekananda

If we think big, we attract greatness to our lives as human beings, beings of light and brotherhood.

Is greatness what you want in your life? Whoever seeks, always finds opportunities!

I remember one of my mentors, Dr. Obom Bowen when he said to me: "What do you want from me? Ask and it will be given to you, you just have to speak and ask, so says God in the bible".

Ask, and it will be given to you; seek, and you will find; knock, and it will be opened to you. For everyone who asks receives, and he who seeks finds, and to him who knocks it will be opened.

Matthew 7:7-11

My response to Dr. Bowen was "I want you to be in my next book, to write the prologue and to join in community".

You and I are blessed because everything we put in affirmation, visualization, and goals always is achieved.

WHEN YOU WANT TO RECEIVE SOMETHING, YOU JUST HAVE TO ASK, THAT IS THE ONLY SECRET OF TRUE SUCCESS.

Today I have started new businesses, conferences, associations, and affiliations because I devote myself to asking, writing, affirming and joining with great people, such as, for example, the author of the prologue of this wonderful book, Analía Exeni, with her *Editorial: Autores de Éxito*; who is my business associate with the Best Seller program.

I also highlight my association with Héctor Rodríguez Curbelo and his network tour *Sé el jefe* (Be the boss) Canada 2020 - 2024.

Be an example of life, vibrating at high frequency, where today is the same as tomorrow, the day after or a hundred days more.

You are the destiny of your life, you are your living book, we are more than conquerors in Jesus Christ, always remember it!

*But we are able to overcome all these things
and more through his love.*

*For I am convinced that neither death nor life,
neither angels nor principalities, neither the
present nor the future, nor any powers, neither
height nor depth, nor anything else in all
creation, will be able to separate us from the
love of God that is in Christ Jesus our Lord.*

Romans 8:37-39

VISUALIZE YOUR SUCCESS.

CREATE YOUR REALITY.

"Positive thinkers create large pictures of what they want in their minds and can predict the future from the present".

Israelmore Ayivor

Changing your character takes time to build new positive thought patterns, to condition your behaviors and therefore your success. The power of self-belief is transmitted to anyone who wants more, wants a favorable change in their life, and looks for different alternatives.

The consistency of positive actions allows to creates an atmosphere of happiness and favorable changes.

I remember a day when I got home after long hours of work, and the excessive time it took me to travel from the west of the city to the east. More than 30 km away and by bus. It was 2 hours of a long journey in the morning and another in the afternoon. More than 4 hours in total. I was disappointed after 8 hours of daily work, after living the same routine every day. However, one day I decided to make a big change. In just one hour I made the decision to make a favorable change to improve my quality of life.

I was totally determined to end my fears and start a new lifestyle. My body and mind told me in unison that it was time for a change. I was the only one able to understand that although I had people watching my efforts every day, they could not feel my frustration or my need for change.

I understood that this decision was mine and no one else's. I decided to break the pattern of fear and get my vehicle the next day, even though I had no driver's license, no training, and not knowing what it is like to drive in detail, but I said to myself, today is the day and that's it! I went to bed, and the next day I got up to go to a car dealership.

Once I got there, I looked around three cars. I sat in a wonderful one with leather seats, and I said to myself, **this is all I need.**

Then I set out to set the terms of the vehicle purchase with the sales representative. The first thing he asked was:

— Could I see your driver's license, please?

I looked at my husband who was next to me. He was speechless, then I replied:

— I do not have a driver's license.

The salesman looked at me desperately confused.

— What? Why?

To which I replied:

— Yes, I don't have yet...

He replied:

 — How many days will it take you to get a driver's license?

— Tomorrow!

He looked at me confused!

— Tomorrow?

I said yes, tomorrow.

I always say that what is important is not what limits you but what you are limited with.

I said: it was long enough! And I proactively worked for change, not looking at the obstacle, but rather at the opportunity for the best change!

I really want you to see in the distance how many things have arrived in your life over the years, you may have experienced pain and losses, but victories have also knocked on your door, your desires are controlled by your destiny, but remember that you are the one who defines what is a need and what is a wish in your life.

When you broadcast the perfect frequency of what you desire, the perfect people, circumstances, and events will be drawn to you and delivered to the energy channel that entered your thoughts through your mind and soul.

Do yourself a favor and watch the instantaneous moments; learn to fail and win; teach your children to dominate their self-love and love for others; respect your desire and feel unstoppable in your actions towards your greatest success. You are the creator of your wealth. Learn to put your trust in God first, then listen to your heartbeat and manifest your condition in things that seem immovable and can be changed in an instant just because you have committed yourself to care and trust.

Put all your hope in God, not looking to your reason for support. In all your ways give ear to him, and he will make straight your footsteps.

Proverbs 3: 5-6

We are definitely not alone. We have the ability to obtain excellent visibility of our future. I can guarantee you that we can get to heaven simultaneously. We have to prepare ourselves to achieve greatness and begin to break the limits and thoughts of poverty, while the changes happen favorably.

My greatest wish is to bring victory to your mind, what is victory? It's you. Yes, you!

No one but YOU deserves the triumph.

The greatest gift in life is being born, and you already have that gift. Enjoy it!

If you face life and it seems that each step you take is more difficult and worsens your situation, remember that the top is heaven, and you are the only one who will reach the top, and that each step you take is a step where you propel with your feet, or you also retract them, that is, you shrink them to go back. The staircase is long, but your thoughts are short when your hope and focus are precise.

Your greatest joy is to see that behind each step you will always have two results: one to improve and another to earn everything you long for every day. Go up! Don't be discouraged! If the struggles seem long, cold and dark, remember that there are others walking up, side by side, and that they also have a destiny, that they will also have failures, and of course stumbles, but that you could always be even better than them.

---

www.breakthroughrose.com

Here you will find a blog aimed at improving your quality of life. Subscribe!

I also invite you to my TV and Radio program *Hablando entre Mujeres* where I will give you Self-Improvement tools. I am waiting for you!

I would like very much you to be part of my YouTube channel: *Rosemarie Sanchez*

MENTALITY IS SPIRITUAL.

"Don't let small minds convince you that your dreams are too big".

Anonymous.

I want to share with you a story that happened many years ago. Are you ready? Very good. Here are some details. I could give you the simple concepts to explain why one more day is so significant, and although time is measured by your own thoughts, it is also important to remember that this ability was created by God for you. It means focusing and reaching a goal, and that goal is based on what you hope to accomplish on the physical plane.

I had the opportunity to meet the Creator of my life, God. I did it when I came to Canada twenty-one years ago.

I looked for help, and help was sent to me, but not as I thought. I got help from people I knew, people that God put into my life. Everything I tried and did was not enough to understand the power of my own actions. I decided to stay in Canada much longer to achieve goals and dreams that I had in mind.

First I had to accept the idea that it would be much more difficult on my own to accomplish a challenge that I needed to justify. My parents and grandmother had invested money, time, and effort, and I appreciated the joy of having the means to pay the cost of tuition, clothing, and accommodation. I realize the challenge of living one day at a time, considering that this was enough to meet my needs, in a place where I was in control of my own life and had to take the risk. Was it simple? Oh no! Was it worth it? Oh yeah! I found everything I needed and felt what I had never felt before in my life, thanks to the blessing of my Lord Jesus Christ. I received everything that my soul and spirit lacked! All this showed me how I had a spiritual thirst to know the truth.

"But I consider my life of no value to myself, if only I may finish my course and complete the ministry I have received from the Lord Jesus— the ministry of testifying to the good news of God's grace".

Acts 20:24

My life was spiritually dead, yet I had a burning desire to have a motivation to create new things internally and externally. I wanted to be someone better and better!

The dream that you have meditated for days, months and years begins to materialize through a positive mindset oriented towards the motivation to achieve the goal.

Is it good to help yourself and not help change other people's lives? Have you heard of the quote "never judge a book by its cover"? That concept definitely changed my mindset.

Conquering a dream where no one but you
are involved is never a dream. This world is
designed to support each other, together
we make a difference! because when we
are united the purpose is complete.

On my website, you will find inspirational
phrases for your life. Visit the website, and
Subscribe.

www.breakthrougrose.com

Chapter 3

DAY-BY-DAY. *"I devour life here and now without leaving for tomorrow what makes me happy today.*

There is no better day than today!
There is no better life than this life.

Yesterday is gone and about tomorrow, we don't know anything. Today is the latent reality!

Are you alive? Do you have air to breathe?
Then you have it all!

There is no better time than this moment…
Remember: life is the biggest prize"

Analía Exeni

TODAY, I want to write this book with one purpose: to show you why every day I felt that my life had a meaning but in a few days I understood that it was real. How much I listened to other mentors has brought different points of view to connect things in my life.

If I had one more day to make a wise decision in my life, that day would be: Today!

I encourage you to make a decision on a personal level, committing yourself to what is right.

There is one thing that all human beings have in common: we need to be appreciated, but not for how much we know, but for how much we can give.

Decide today to make a change that fills your spirit with inner peace; Make a great decision that determines radical improvements in your life.

"Let me embrace thee, sour adversity, for wise men say it is the wisest course."

William Shakespeare.

Looking through my rear mirror, there is a past to remember. It is also necessary to appreciate how much I have achieved so far and to know with total conviction that **my future is unlimited.**

Every step you take shapes your destiny. Of course you want to be a better person every day, but staying in the comfort zone makes you feel happy and uncomfortable at the same time. You as an entrepreneur in your life know that **risk is a daily choice, ups and downs are the virtue of your destiny**, because they allow you to change the control pattern of your mind, building new thoughts that favor you.

Knowledge is not enough if it is not accompanied by ACTION.

One day at a time, seems too little or too much? What do you think?

I know that my destiny is older than me. I hope to enjoy each chapter of this book expressing how **changing the pattern of poverty** has controlled humanity to achieve greatness. So, stop thinking that your world is not changing. If you are uncomfortable with your energy, it is because something is happening on the spiritual plane. God is awakening the wish to believe more, love more, dream more. We

must hope that our future ahead will be better
and better, and surely it will be!

*"He can who thinks he can, and he can't who
thinks he can't. This is an inexorable,
indisputable law".*

Pablo Picasso

You will find a special blog with messages that
inspire your life on my website:
www.breakthroughrose.com

YOUR SOUL SHOWS YOUR BRIGHTNESS.

"Beauty is a radiance that originates from within and comes from inner security and strong character".

Jane Seymour

Have your expressions ever shown the meaning of your thoughts?

With a strong character, the unimaginable is achieved.

Whenever I walk into an empty place and start interacting, whether it's asking any questions, or asking for a purchase order, or even choosing a product for sale, many people start walking into the place and space fills up.

104

Do you think it's luck? Well, let me tell you it's not like that.

When your spirit has been built to have a stronger character, your radiance becomes noticeable, your light is greater than your thoughts.

Then you become a blessing magnet for others.

May the light of the Lord's face be shining on you in grace".
Numbers 6:25

I can pursue a dream, because the radiance of God and his virtue shine on me, illuminate me and my soul feels motivated towards more spiritual things that fulfill my life with abundance.

I remember when I was a girl and sometimes I felt unable to understand the big people who with their behavior did not give an example of what they taught or preached. I used to look for more answers and a role model to base my opinions on. Although I was not sure of my character, I understood that the more I concentrated my energy on the positive, I could prevent many people from thinking about me incorrectly. **Tolerance always teaches us a lesson.**

"Children must have a lot of tolerance with adults."

Antoine de Saint-Exupéry

Have you noticed something interesting on a train? Have you been to a station waiting for the train to arrive and as you approached the station did you notice that it didn't stop? Now imagine that all you see is the light from the booths flickering through your eyes. The same concept is your radiance, because it is unattainable. Many people long for it, but only a few will walk in the train cabins, which is your life. Because each cabin can be defined as:

- Your attitude
- Your unique talents
- Your spirituality
- Your integrity
- Your ethical actions
- Your words of encouragement
- The love that reflects your heart, etc.

Would you let all your qualities be on board with you? Would you choose to make a difference with the people who trusted you and entered your train cabins? Would you hide the magnitude of your achievements and the glow of those train cabins of your life in the dark?

If you want abundance in your life you must show your radiance. You must show people that you are a trustworthy person. This is a principle of all the laws of the universe.

One thing that all human beings have in common throughout human history is compassion. Your spirit is a radiance of this feeling. Even the meanest person on earth will fear at some point and bow down showing compassion and pity, therefore, make a choice: that today it is your inner glow that overcomes everything, you will always see the door open, you will find people who will follow and respect you, because you have transformed your attitude through your radiance in abundance.

"Darkness cannot drive out darkness: only light can do that. Hate cannot drive out hate: only love can do that".

Martin Luther King, Jr.

I invest my time in people like you, who want to excel and grow in all areas, breaking barriers and changing patterns that have not allowed you to reach your most appreciated destination, **approaching you to that great person who is you in fullness.**

Please visit my website: www.breakthroughrose.com, and sign up for information about tutoring.

THE PEACE OF THE HEART FERTILIZES NEW SOIL.

"Start by doing what is necessary, then what is possible, and suddenly you are doing the impossible".

St. Francis of Assisi

The world progresses in chaos every day. It is irreversible, and unfortunately, I doubt it will change...

What can you do to reverse this chaos?

Your heart can work harder every day looking for a way to bring peace; looking for a way to force your mentality to control your outside world in alignment with your own being, seeking the truth beyond any reasonable human being and working for it.

I have cultivated my relationship with God in the deepest and highest love, love that transcends the reasoning of every person in this world.

Maybe you have not yet managed to get your heart to the fertile land of peace, but you must not give up, you must fight your own demons with all your strength, and if that is not enough, it is because what governs the world has to change from the carnal enjoyment to the deepest of the spirit.

You must contribute! Bring your grain of sand to build a world full of peace.

Peace will allow your heart to bring to the world a new spiritual human being, to create on earth, in your earth! a clean and pure stage.

I wonder if any of you who read this book will seek to mature in a relationship of love and integrity within your heart and between people with the same vision of life. But we have not yet realized that the human mind has not processed it to achieve it. That is why the heart needs to be above the level of resignation, with no regrets.

It is a bit difficult to understand these kinds of things so profound when we are so hurried and stressed in life, without analyzing the scope and importance of having peace of heart.

When things go wrong, you can deny the fact that your heart is in adversity, you can even think that cooperating with the situation you are handling may soon bring you to the end of that adversity. This is likely to be possible, certainly time and effort will reward you.

But what ends physically in your sight, can also demand a change in your heart and if this process is not healed, I guarantee that the same situation can happen again in one way or another, so that your eyes see it in different circumstances, but it will definitely be described in your life as a need for a change in you, in order to bring a new beginning, a new land to your land and to fruitfully develop new seeds, which will continue to lead you in a direction to achieve peace in you.

Happiness is a state of mind while peace is in the spirit and in alignment with your soul, mind, spirit, heart, and body.

Feed those friends and people who have come to you to help with your blessings continually. Be grateful to those who helped you be happier.

Keep building the unannounced events that will allow to your spirit the freedom. It is unforgivable, because even thinking that it was not prepared to happen, still our energy and thoughts created it. That is the existence to surround us with time. It had already passed, even healed, and it is not within our stigma and it will not be in you either.

"Someday, somewhere, anywhere, unfailingly, you'll find yourself, and that, and only that, can be the happiest or bitterest hour of your life".

Pablo Neruda

DO YOU MASTER THE ECONOMY?

"It's more important to grow your income than cut your expenses.

It's more important to grow your spirit that cut your dreams".

Robert Kiyosaki

People have changed the economy with movements to grow money more effectively with digital ads, the media, and investment portfolios. While society is changing rapidly, millennials also have more opportunities than ever to work in whatever industry they choose.

Why do many people wisely seek high-level business?

It's a great time to do things differently, technology is changing every industry and now people are no longer looking for a single source of income, and they shouldn't be either.

Every entrepreneur working with the financial, healthcare and consumer industries today has become more aware of how relationships impact the different goals each individual has in mind.

To benefit from the economy as a powerful source of income, businesses will have to be developed strategically, somewhat differently, and by looking at what the competition is doing in the industry they want to belong to.

I have watched closely the people who were trained through financial advisors. Mentors and leaders in any industry have had the opportunity to choose a different path to success, although their beliefs have been raised to make a difference and to make their own decisions based on their needs.

I'm going to testify what my mother experienced! She had a great lesson. When she realized that she had not had the correct financial education and the wrong information or the right sources, she invested her money wrongly and not wisely. As a result, I decided to help her change that pattern and push her toward that change. I also educated myself financially to manage my business in accordance with what the economy demands, knowing that its regulations could potentially help me in the process of investing wisely and getting correct directions for my financial future towards prosperity.

I admire people who have invested their time and effort to manage their financial lives by listening and approaching the strategies given by experts in the field, achieving a financial GPS, which means having a roadmap to their final destination for retirement and dreams to achieve.

"Failure will never overtake me if my determination to succeed is strong enough".

Og Mandino

People do not plan to fail, they fail without the plan executed. Why? Precisely because fear of failure is greater than positive thoughts and determination to conquer a result that favors their needs.

If you seek, you will also find.

Never underestimate your priorities for faith or the fulfillment of what you have created. A challenge is always a step to a door that opens with courage and determination. You can master your ideas and principles whenever you need it.

In addition, the economy in each and every one of these days is evolving for better or for worse, but you have the potential to change from zero to magnitudes. Remember that everything is in you. Could someone else have the responsibility?

You are the Artist and Author of your life, define it for good always!

WHAT IS THE RIGHT ANSWER?

"Never give up. Your call is one step ahead, hold on and reach your full potential"

Rosemarie Sánchez

A girl named Marie had won many Olympic Games, obtaining countless medals, but despite the certainty of her success, she kept looking for answers. Have you ever wondered what is beyond success? This question had remained in Marie's mind for years.

Should this be the end of her career? She knew that any answer would be uncertain at the age of twenty.

She has been a determined young woman for high-level sport, but she always kept her personal dreams hidden.

As you can see, this girl who had achieved a life of challenges still showed that in her mind she had doubts about her destiny.

When meeting Juan in a boulevard, Marie was very afraid that he would see her. She had no confidence in herself. But how is it that a winner of many medals and trophies has patterns of incarceration when interacting with others? It is a very complex question.

Juan is another athlete with the same skills and similar awards, who also gave up his

childhood to become an athlete, deprived of
his adolescence, of enjoying with friends,
going to the movies, etc. There is an answer to
this: discipline has governed their lives since
they were children, because their parents saw
in them a great talent.

Marie never grew up among children, she
didn´t learn to behave like one of them, she
did not attend school. Her very protective
family, eager to make her a *star*, took her
away from that world to keep her motivated to
conquer her career as an athlete, always
demanding her to exceed the next level of
excellence.

They forced her to follow strict schedules and
routines with the sole purpose that Marie could
become a champion. That was exactly the
wish of her parents, that the girl had a career

as a professional tennis player, which she achieved and exceded.

Is it possible that a child is determined to win each and every one of his games without accepting defeats?

Do you identify yourself in this situation?

Have you already discovered your passion and love for life?

Has anyone approached you with a significant desire to help you, and give you feedback on what you should do based on your perspective?

So if your *self belief* and passion has been revealed over time, you can have the right answer that applies to your determination to succeed, to change and improve your world. But it may also be that defeat leads you to the beginning of a better path of success 100% created by you.

A writer said:

"Unless you try to do something beyond what you have already mastered, you will never grow".

Unknown.

Definitely infinite love to achieve goals and dreams must be the answer to your questions.

What is important is not what others want from you, what is important is what makes you happy. You have the leading role in all this, and that's when you must understand that the approval of others is not always important; in many cases, it is better to stay away from the addiction of pleasing

others and fundamentally learning to stop and SAY NO!

The ideas that God has placed in your heart and soul continue to grow every day. Tomorrow the sun will shine or shadows will set around it, thus having a less bright day. Still, you must keep your motivation intact, create synergy with the shadows, and allow yourself to continue on your way to your best destination.

MANIFEST THE CHANGE OUTSIDE OF YOU.

"What makes you great as a human being, and therefore rich, are your personal values, because your values elevate you above all the mediocrity in the world making you a millionaire".

Analía Exeni.

What is the greatness of this book? I'm going to explain to you the revelation of wonderful things that happened in the past.

When you look back, you admire yourself, because your today has changed; you come to realize the manifestation of God in your life.

Every day, permanently, I had to look for more. My soul was empty because my purpose was not revealed to me for long, because I first dedicated my life to pleasing others before pleasing my own needs. My self-esteem was not clear to me. I knew about my strong personality, but also how weak I felt when saying *NO* to people.

People who seek to *please everyone* will always find emptiness in their hearts and loneliness on their way.

One day I met a friend who I had not seen in a long time. We agreed to see each other, but when talking with him I realized that our needs were totally different and our desires were totally opposite. I could immediately see how time had separated us and how different our lives were. Our interests were not the same.

My beliefs and needs were certainly from another planet for him, but very real for me, because my criteria of life were designed to help people, yet he was still arrogant and selfish. I wondered, what changed? If we both grew up together we did the same things we had the same interests.

The answer came to me immediately. I realized that there was a very different light in me than his, because it had changed my perspective of finding the way for my own good. But I still wasn't able to say NO to what was inappropriate for my time and needs. God had manifested grace in me, so my thoughts began to change positively. I gave myself up to seek my entrepreneurial spirit. I received my call!

I found what I needed: my trust in Christ and in myself, the meaning and purpose of my Kingdom. Why my Kingdom? Because God had revealed himself to me and now I have the strength to walk in infinite grace. I see people with dignity and also mercy. I see the way that God sees me. Is it possible to achieve all this happiness? Yes! You just have to declare every daily victory over every episode in your life.

Favorable changes will occur to those who patiently wait and fulfill their calling in life.

It doesn't matter how mistreated you have been; how much injustice you have faced. Challenges will always define your true identity.

An eagle can fly through the storm, through strong winds and terrible storms; It even flies higher than all the birds in the world, it is never afraid of the dark. It achieves greatness because as the storm hits it overcomes all the obstacles it faces with great determination. When it rests, it goes to the top of the mountain to admire the beauty of life, the majestic nature. The eagles will declare victory once the storm has stopped. You can do the same, too, even if storms hit you against the toughest rocks of your life. Winds can knock you to the ground, but if your wings are still open you will be ready for a new flight.

You will always have the power to face circumstances. I also have that power; all human beings have it.

Be an eagle that never fears darkness because the light is on you.

"When there is a storm the birds hide, but the eagles fly higher".

Mahatma Gandhi

Pray in difficult times and seek peace in your heart. Remain alert in anguish, using prayer as the best weapon in the face of unforeseen events and adversities.

We are spirit and flesh. Our war is spiritual and will manifest in our physical universe.

You also have the strength through your thoughts to send love, doubts and uncertainty, you are also able to know when you can throw away everything that is not making you grow.

*"I will never let anyone walk through my mind
with their dirty feet".*

Mahatma Gandhi

Be Strong as the eagle!

Forgiveness is always at your disposal, just love with all your strength and love will find the forgiveness you long for.

Lower your weapons and let the eagle rush to get there faster than the wind itself.

Be Humble!

Because if we are sure of something, it is that we will leave this land called fertile, but sterile inside. Don't be the eagle that reaches the finish line and says "I already did it. There are no more storms, I can only wait to tea so that the wind I suffered for every flight I tried never knocks on my door and it always manifested itself as simple as the aura in the sea".

Today you are in time that each dream, each sigh and each infinity are only what you most long to be. To be that flower that is reborn and stops fading because of the water that never reached it.

When they go into the tent of meeting, they shall wash with water, that they die not; or when they come near to the altar to minister, to burn an offering made by fire unto Jehovah. So they shall wash their hands and their feet, that they die not: and it shall be a statute forever to them, even to him and to his seed throughout their generations.

Exodus 30:20-21

If you liked this book, please leave a positive comment at:

Amazon

Send me a message on my website:

www.breakthroughrose.com

You can sign up and get 30 minutes of free tutoring.

ROSEMARIE

Roses always form between the thorns; the thorns always form from each branch in transition.

Good times **O**scillate in my mind I know that you also feel the same. We are always energy!

Sow each rose in fertile soil, never stop endure the solid soil that God gave you. We are victory!

I am h**e**re and I value every gift I have and I serve daily. I am a miracle on the move to success!

Mentioning a little more of everything I am is simple, with a single phrase I can express it, I am exactly what God gave me, life on the move!

Attend every thought to supernaturally way. It is in your mind to react intentionally or carelessly. Today I make the decision to do things better in my circle of experiences forever.

I laugh every sunrise as I look at the sun and say, "Thank you, God, that you are always present in my life.

Individually we are able to be more aware of our truth, let us be light and not darkness.

I understand that being Rosemarie is being a Rose in my own life because I am Marie of goodness and truth.

I am full of love and blessing

For ever!

Acknowledgements

So much to be thanked for and so much to mention. My heart is overjoyed. Firstly, this book has been done with great effort. I need to thank God first. He is my engine, and he is everything in me. Thank you, Christ, because you have made all your perfect plans in me.

First of all, I thank all the people who have trusted me. I start by thanking Analía Exeni who said this book is a BEST SELLER and I will never doubt her abilities and talent gave me the joy of showing this masterpiece to the world. Thanks Analía for being a great coach *Writers Coach* with your *Academy Autores de Éxito*. I bless you infinitely, thank you for writing the wonderful prologue made for the world and myself.

I thank my Grandmother, Lucila Velásquez, who always saw in me the pattern to follow generations of conquest. She said "you will follow in my footsteps" and now I understand. Olga Lucila Velázquez with more than 30 Science and Poetry books, made books for the greatness of the soul, thank you Grandma! Because you have been an example of life in my life.

I am infinitely grateful to my life mentors, James MacNeil, Emilio Román, Daniela Román, Héctor

Rodríguez Curbelo, Dr. Bom Bowen, Raymond Aaron, Dilesh Bhullar, Laila Bhullar, Daniel Pirillo.

To my friends colleagues, Jorge de Jesús Núñez García who is a Journalist and radio announcer with his *Radio station Urbanatvfm* and his program *Panorama Hispano* and *KBDTO*. María Ocampo, Joseph Jiménez with *Frequency5fm*, the production of *2ENLINEA TV*. Kirsty Seferina for her support in communication networks. Wilder M Gómez, Juan Alberto Silva for transmitting on *Al día Radio station* my program *Hablando entre Mujeres*. William Jiménez Rozo Journalist and radio announcer for *Magazin Sin Fronteras*, Hugo Hernández of *Universus Radio* for being my best friend, colleague, journalist and radio announcer. Oscar Palomino Rodríguez as director and founder of the radio station *Impacto FM station*, for transmitting my program in Colombia, to all of them thank you, and infinite successes.

A special thanks to Mariana Santos, who is my kindred spirit, Author of the book that united our lives *Spiritual Fitness Survivor*, also colleague with her Immigration program, *Santos & Associates immigration Inc.*, for all our experiences, for giving me strength in crucial moments of my life. Thank you Mariana, for making dreams come true for each immigrant who is your client and makes Canada the country of their lives with your excellent services. I bless you infinitely!

To Laurie K. Grant who has been a part of my life, giving me so much in such a short time. I thank you who put your love, support, and trust in this book, I say to you thank you very much and I wish that this legacy always means a lot of success for you in everything you undertake. Blessings!

To Marta Huerta and Ramón González of the company *contracorriente.com*, from Madrid, Spain, who designed the cover and back cover of this book, to you my sincerest thanks for such majestic work. Blessings!

To Tony Romo, I thank you for your professional work in the banner designs for my events with *Puffin Marketing*. Thank you so much. Keep being the leader you are!

My friend Ben Anthony *La Voz* and who I had and have had the honor to train his mind, I admire your work Ben, thanks for trusting me.

To Ámbar Michelangeli the kindred spirit of my childhood and adolescence, that has always been in my life for years.

To my friends and colleagues in Mexico: Juan Nila Pérez, Israel Ayezer, Gloria Hekker producer and radio announcer; as well as so many others with whom I am infinitely grateful for your help and brotherhood, thank you all for being present in my life. I love Mexico, I bless you infinitely!

To my friends that I have in the Christian group *Construyendo Juntas* to each one of you, thank you for your support and strength to my soul. Blessings!

To my direct and indirect family, to all those who are near and far, it would be too much to tell so much love from my Sánchez family and my Carmona family. I love you very much. The happiness of being a family is infinite. Thank you, I bless you all!

Thanks to Mauricio Jiménez for always having sponsored my professional photos and your distinguished work with *Magic Vision* is of real value to my life and that of anyone who seeks your services. Thank you I bless you!

I want to bless and thank all the beloved public that follows my program *Hablando entre Mujeres* that has impacted many lives and I have had the opportunity to interview personalities like writers, artists, and influencers for the Hispanic and Anglo-Saxon community in Canada, with their life and professional experiences. Thank you for always being part of the program and believing in me. I bless you!

To the group of extraordinary women *RIMLA International* that we conform a group of victorious entrepreneurs, bringing radical changes to the world. United, we can do everything!

To the organization *S.O.S. Peace*, to its President Antonio Carlos C. Silveira, Latin American Ambassador Susana Moya, To José Lucas Ambassador of the world and singer-songwriter, executive producers Glen Vargas and Vandim Productions; with the production of the song *Canto por la Paz*, which has been a big success in the world. Thank you for giving my life the step to artistic singing, as well as I appreciate the work done in Mexico by Executive Director Gabriela Alcantar and I thank you for choosing me as Executive Director in Canada. To all this organization I thank you for trusting me and valuing my work for humanity. I bless each one of you!

To the group of *Unstoppable Women* that we are more than 20 women all for a cause and doing much more together. Thank you and I bless you always!

To all my friends, colleagues, writers, and representatives not mentioned here, but you know I mean you. Thank you because I have had the happiness to know each one of you and have your love and fraternity.

The list is long but here the protagonist is you. Let's keep building! we are more than conquerors!

"Accustom yourself continually to make many acts of love, for they enkindle and melt the soul".

Saint Teresa of Avila

Author's Biography

Rosemarie Sánchez, author Best Seller International # 1 twice, with the books *Spiritual Fitness Survivor*, in collaboration with 26 authors, being awarded for this masterpiece and *Magnetic Entrepreneur* with the participation of more than 125 authors and their Biography, this book broke the World Guinness Record, where all the participants signed the book simultaneously.

Professional speaker for personal development and business strategies, professional Singer. She has a degree in accounting, Investments and insurance agent in Canada. Latin Award Canada nominated Rosemarie in 2019 like Artist of the Year in Christian Music, with the song *Canto por la Paz*; She is the executive director of the *NGO S.O.S. Peace* in Canada.

Rosemarie resides in Toronto, Canada for over 21 years working with the Latino community. In the same way, she has produced events with: *JEP Agency*, for Miss Canada Latina 2015 and is part of the Miss Teen Universe Canada Organization, as executive director of marketing and business. She is a radio and television presenter with her program: *Hablando entre mujeres*, which it has been transmitted by *2ENLINEA TV*, *Frequency5fm*, *Al Día Radio*, *Universus Radio*, *Urbanatvfm* and *Impactofmestero* as well as digital media, like Facebook, Instagram and YouTube. She has worked in such movies as *Shazam* and *Downsizing* next to Matt Damon in two scenes.

This book *Quebrando Barreras*, changing the pattern of poverty, will be translated into English with the title: *BREAKTHROUGH* and subtitle: *Changing the Pattern of Poverty*, that addresses the topics of emotional, spiritual, physical, and financial intelligence, and will also be awarded for its content. This book will be published in 2020 in English once this Spanish version is published by *Autores de Éxito*, with the prologue by Analía Exeni, # 1 International Best Seller Author with her book *Mujer Imparable*, this book has Rosemarie Sánchez participation in the prologue, praising the work of Analía Exeni, that book became # 1

International Best Seller Author in the USA, CANADA and SPAIN on Amazon.

Rosemarie is working to release her first album with music by different artists in Spanish and English and also with duets and other voices for the songs on her first CD.

Rosemarie is the founder and president of the event company *Breakthroughrose Productions*. She has performed *Song for Peace* with James MacNeil at the end of the song in English.

Canto por la Paz is a song dedicated to humanity, for children in war and terrorism. We need to bring a revival to the world, that is the commitment of many singers who are singing this song by José Lucas, who is a singer-songwriter, and Glen Vargas who is in charge of the production of the song, is the anthem of the *NGO SOS Peace*.

Rosemarie has been coached by several people who teach business at a high level and professional and personal growth such as James MacNeil, Raymond

Aaron, Dr. Obom Bowen, Héctor Rodríguez Curbelo among others.

That is why she has developed skills in personal training and international business.

Her Social Media are:

Rosemarie Sánchez

- http://www.breakthroughrose.com
- rose@breakthroughrose.com
- Instagram: @breakthroughrose
- Facebook: Rosemarie Sanchez
- Facebook: Breakthroughrose
- WhatsApp +1-416-837-6647
- Phone: +1 647-977-0144

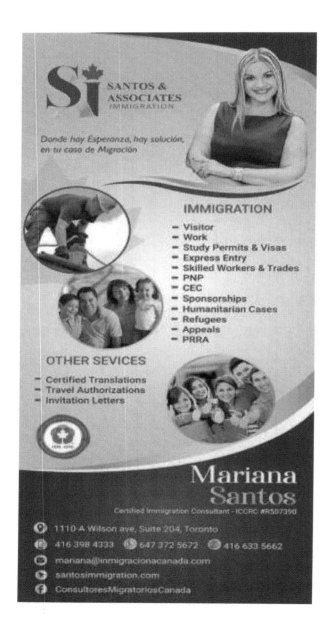

EFFECTIVE MESSAGING FOR SUCCESS

Laurie K. Grant
DIGITAL TRANSFORMATIONS

CALL SHYUI

3M Web Design, Content Magic
Social Marketing
Business Illumination

1-416-949-4926
shyuidigital@gmail.com
SHYUI.COM

Laurie K. Grant is a successful business consultant, speaker, author and business thought leader.

SHYUI (shy you i), a division of her company, FutureWave Group, provides Digital Transformations focused on 3M Web Design, Content Magic, Social Marketing and Business Illumination for Businesses who want to effectively highlight their messaging.

Don't Be Shy

CALL SHYUI

For Your Digital

Transformation

TODAY!!

Made in the USA
Columbia, SC
30 September 2020